75P

Animals
and
Insects

UNDER THE MICROSCOPE

Animals
and
Insects
UNDER THE MICROSCOPE

John Woodward & Casey Horton

Blitz Editions

This edition published in 1996 by
Blitz Editions
an imprint of Bookmart Ltd
Registered number 2372865
Trading as Bookmart Ltd
Desford Road
Enderby
Leicester LE9 5AD

ISBN: 1-85605-364-4

Editorial and design: Brown Packaging Books Ltd
255-257 Liverpool Road
London N1 1LX

Printed in Italy

Picture credits
The publishers would like to thank the Science Photo Library for supplying
all of the photographs used in this book, except the following:
page 19: Natural History Photographic Agency
pages 29, 35: Frank Lane Picture Agency
page 39: Tony Stone Images

CONTENTS

FLEA CIRCUS

Fleas are insects and they are pests. They spend most of their lives living on other animals. In fact, fleas would die out if they could not do this. They are parasites, and they need other animals for food. Adult fleas suck blood. They have a very sharp 'tube' – called a proboscis – on their head, which pierces through the victim's skin and draws the blood up into the mouth. A special substance in the flea's saliva goes down the proboscis and into the animal. This substance stops the blood from clotting. The larva of the dog flea lives on debris and adult flea droppings.

In this picture of a dog flea you can see the hard plates, or shields, that cover its body. You can also see the sharp proboscis, which it uses to pierce the dog's skin.

WITH A HOP, SKIP AND A JUMP

- Although they are troublesome, fleas are amazing insects. They cannot fly, but they hop and skip – and they can jump distances more than 80 times their own height. If a man 2 metres tall could jump this far he would be able to leap 160 metres in one bound!

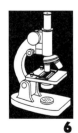

MOUTH ORGAN

The tongue is made up of muscles. Some muscles change the shape of the tongue. Others change the position of the tongue in the mouth. Most animals have tongues, and many of them – including humans – use their tongues for swallowing and tasting food. Taste buds, scattered over the surface of the tongue, tell us whether foods are salty, sour, sweet or bitter. The cells in each taste bud are linked to nerve cells that send 'taste' messages to the brain.

The taste buds on this animal's tongue can be seen on either side of the long groove that runs down the centre of the picture. Each taste bud contains many cells.

PROVE IT YOURSELF

- The taste buds for sweet, sour, salty and bitter are in different places on the tongue. You can find out where they are. Put a tiny drop of vinegar on your finger. Now touch the tip, the side and the back of your tongue. Where could you taste the sour vinegar? Try this experiment with sugar (sweet), salt, and vanilla extract (bitter).

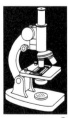

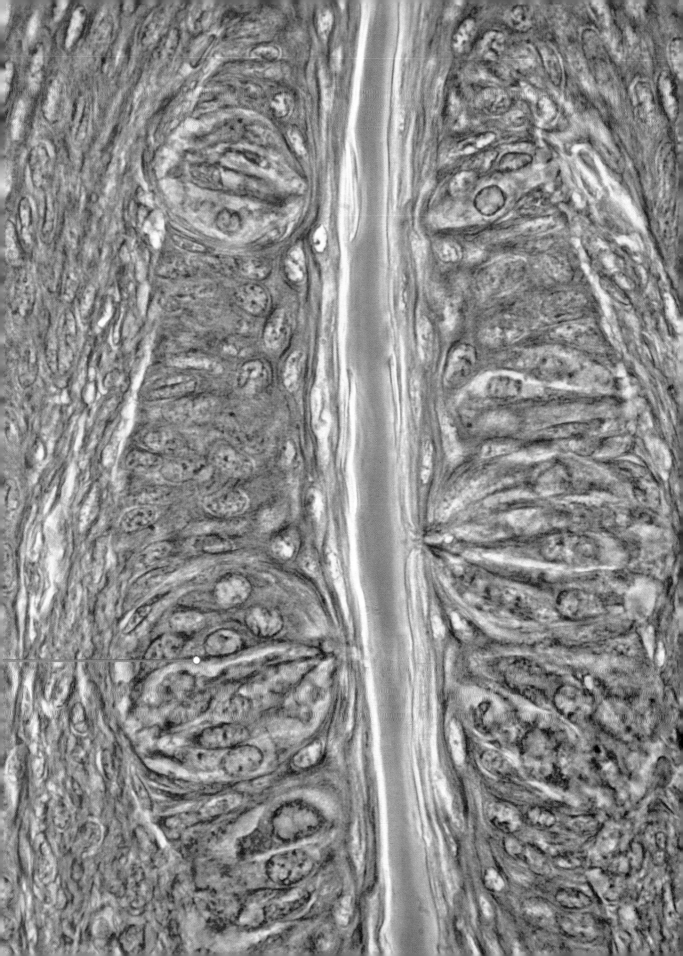

ABSORBING FOOD

The intestine is the main part of the body where food is broken down, or digested, into substances that can be used by the body. It is divided into two basic parts: the small and the large intestine. Once food leaves the stomach it goes into the small intestine. Here most of the food is dissolved in a liquid. The wall of the small intestine is folded – like the folds of a curtain, or the pleats of an accordion – and is lined with millions of very small finger-like structures called villi. The villi contain tiny blood vessels, called capillaries. These absorb the dissolved food, which is carried in the blood to other parts of the body.

The finger-like orange structures in this photograph are the villi in the intestine of a mouse. The green matter is the waste material left over after the food has been broken down.

THE LONG AND THE SHORT OF IT

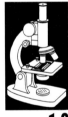

- In a full-grown human adult, the small intestine is about 7–7.5 metres long. The large intestine measures about 1.5 metres in length.

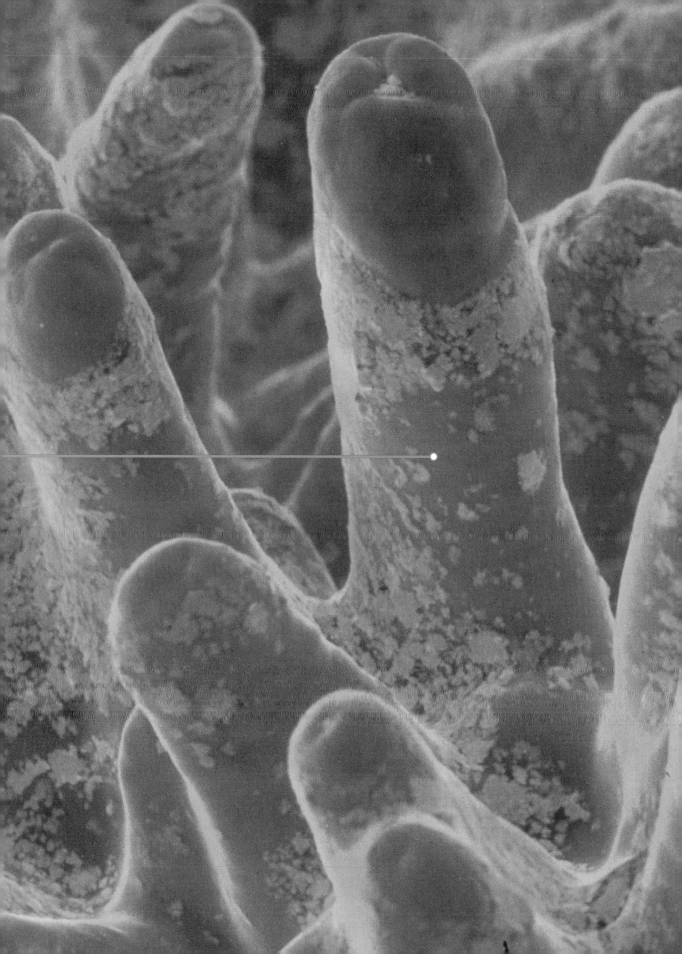

LICKING INTO SHAPE

If you have a pet cat you will know it uses its tongue for grooming and eating. When a cat is drinking milk it curls up the end of its tongue to make a shallow bowl. The cat laps up the milk by moving its tongue in and out very quickly. Hooked knobs, called papillae, lie in the centre of the tongue. You can feel these when a cat licks your skin. They feel rough, like sandpaper. The way a cat's tongue is attached in its mouth determines whether it can roar or purr. For example, tigers can roar but not purr, while pet cats can purr but not roar.

Here you can see why a cat's tongue feels so rough. These are the hooked papillae on the cat's tongue. They act like a comb when the cat grooms its fur.

CLEAN AS A WHISTLE

- Cats don't only groom themselves to keep clean. When the cat licks itself it spreads saliva on its fur. The saliva evaporates and this helps to keep the cat cool. Licking also releases oils from special glands in the skin. The oil keeps the cat's fur waterproof.

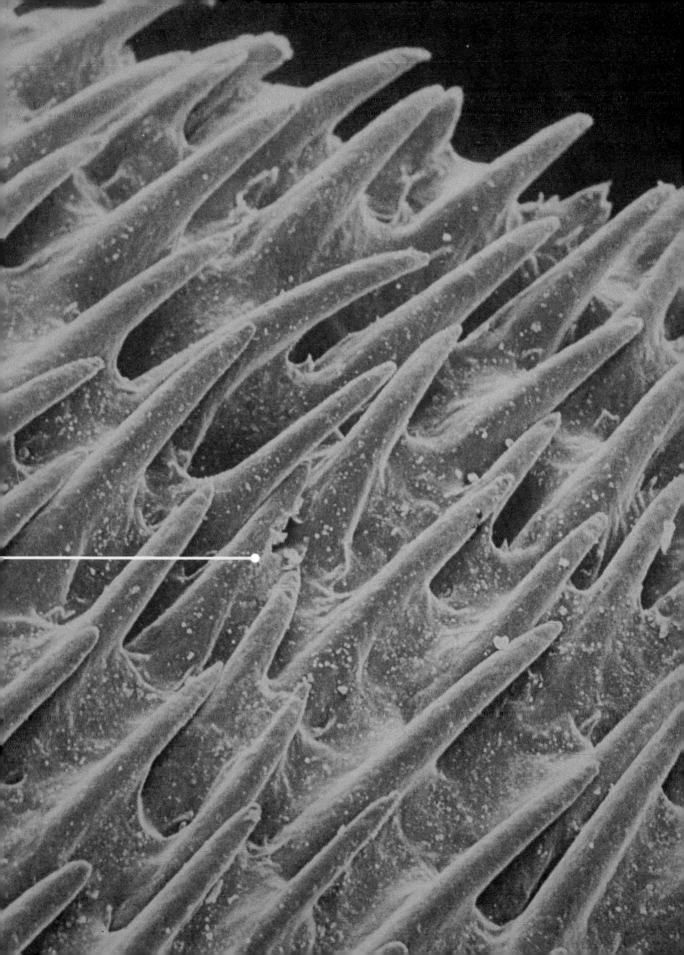

WARMING WOOL

Wool is a type of hair that comes from sheep and some other animals. Domesticated sheep have two kinds of wool: thin, softer wool that lies close to the skin, and a coat of longer, thicker wool on top. The thicker, outer wool helps to protect the sheep and keep it warm. It can keep humans warm too, when it is knitted or woven into fabric and made into clothes. Both hair and wool are covered with scales. Hair has scales that are flat and overlap each other rather like the petals of a rose. The scales on a fibre of wool are pointed and form a honeycomb pattern.

In this photograph of wool fibres, taken from a domestic sheep, you can see clearly the honeycomb pattern of scales on the thick fibres in the foreground.

WOOLLY FACTS

• Ranchers in the United States raise about 10 million sheep, which give some 40 million kilograms of wool every year. The leading sheep-rearing states include Texas, California, South Dakota, New Mexico, and Wyoming.

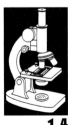

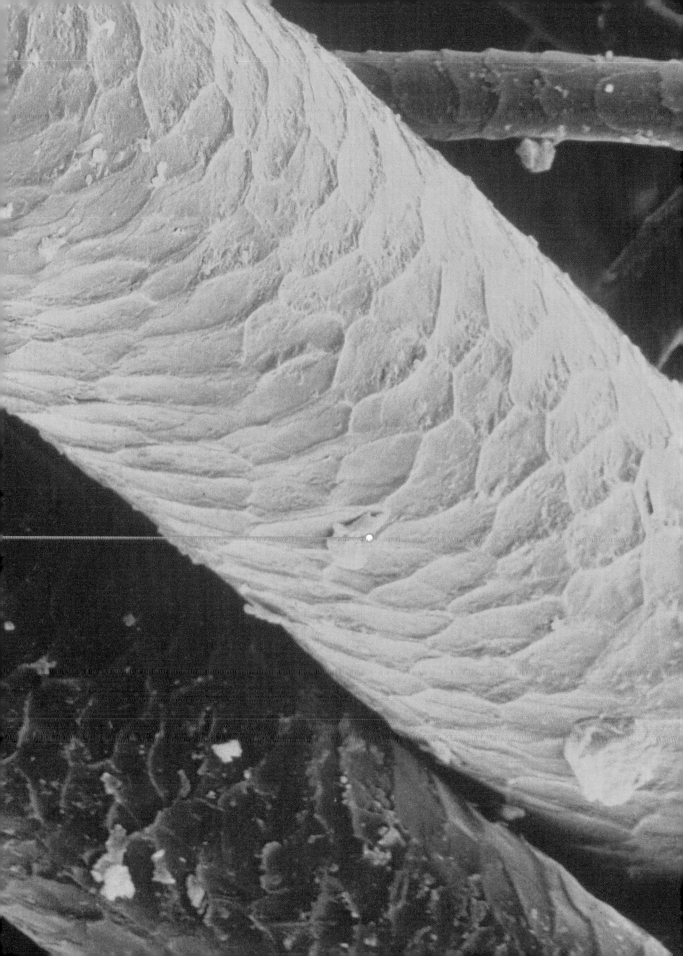

TIGHT SQUEEZE

The python is a killer snake, but it does not kill by poisoning. It coils its long body around the animal it has caught and squeezes until the animal can no longer breathe. It holds on while it pushes the dead animal into its mouth. The python lies in wait for its prey and then springs out, knocking the animal off balance. The Indian python lives near water. It is a good swimmer and can also climb trees. Like other pythons it attacks and eats mammals such as cats, dogs and rats, and birds such as pigeons and ducks.

A snake's body is covered with horny, overlapping scales. The scales in this picture belong to an Indian python. Although snakes look slimy, their scales are quite dry.

MOTHER LOVE?

• The Indian python grows to a length of 6 metres. When the female has laid her clutch of 100 eggs she wraps her long body around them. She incubates the eggs for two to three months, until the young snakes hatch. During this time she leaves them only to take a drink and, sometimes, to eat.

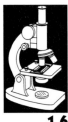

MINI DINOSAUR

The iguana is a lizard. Some people think it looks like a miniature dinosaur. It has four legs and a long tail, and its skin is covered with overlapping scales. On parts of the body these scales are shaped into crests and spines. For example, the green iguana has a spiky crest that runs from its head down to its tail. Many iguanas have flaps of skin hanging around their head and neck. Most iguanas live on land. Some live in forests, or very near them, and are good at climbing trees. Other iguanas live on rocky coasts near the sea and are excellent swimmers.

Iguanas do not have an outer ear like we do. As you can see here, the ear opens directly into the head. The dark area in the centre of the picture is the ear drum.

FREE FALL

• Green iguanas live in the tropics, near tropical forests. When climbing trees they often go as high as 12–15 metres above the ground. Sometimes they leap down to the ground from high branches. Amazingly, they walk away completely unhurt.

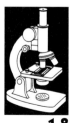

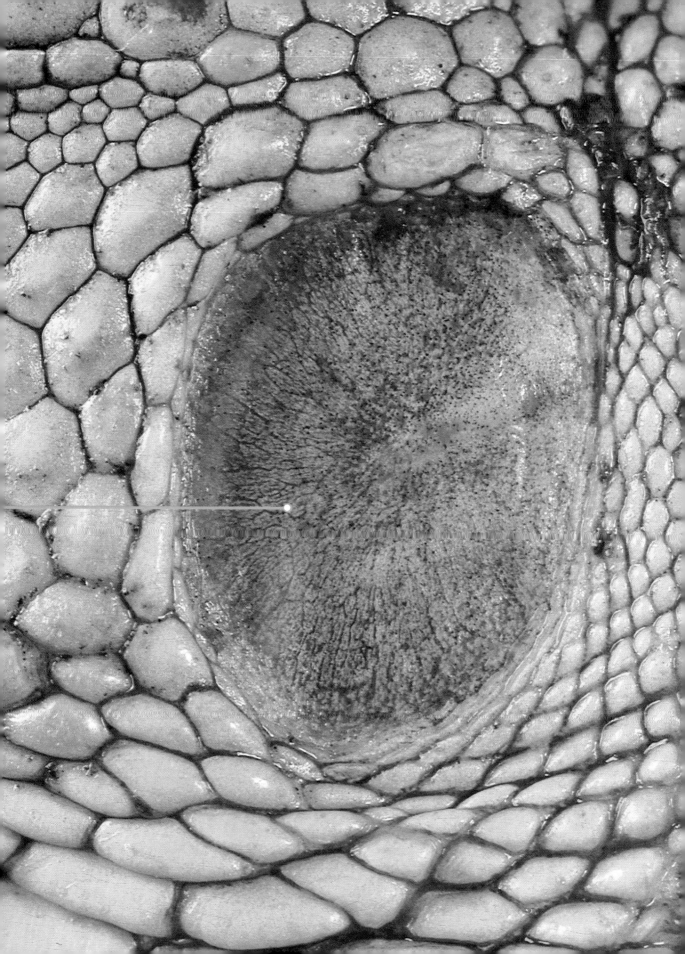

FEATHER WEIGHT

People often use the phrase 'as light as a feather' to describe how little something weighs. And feathers really are very light. However, they are also very strong. The central part of the feather – called the shaft – is hollow at the end nearest the body. It grows from a small bud in the bird's skin. Very fine filaments, called barbs, grow from each side of the shaft. Each barb has two rows of small side branches, called barbules. The barbules on one side have hooks, and the ones on the other side have grooves. The hooks and grooves fit together like velcro to make a flat surface, called the vane.

The feather in this picture originally belonged to a magpie. The thick, blue-gray lines you can see are the barbs, and the fine yellow strands are the barbules.

SOLVE THIS PUZZLE!

- Which is heavier – a kilogram of feathers or a kilogram of potatoes? See if you can find the answer to this curious question.

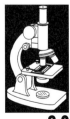

FUR COATS

Dogs, like many other mammals, have two kinds of hair on their body. Long, rather coarse hairs, called guard hairs, protect softer, shorter hairs underneath. These hairs trap still air close to the skin, helping the dog keep warm. Humans lose some of their hairs throughout the year, as do some other animals. But animals that live in places with hot or warm summers and cold winters lose a lot of their hair all at once. When winter has passed and the temperature rises, dogs moult. Their coats become thinner in preparation for the hot summer weather.

In this picture you can clearly see the lumps of dandruff clinging to a dog's hair. This hair was photographed in a piece of house dust.

WHITE FOXES

- The Arctic fox is a type of wild dog that lives near the North Pole. In summer its coat is coloured greyish-yellow. But when the deep snows of winter come to the Arctic the hairs in the fox's coat become pure white, like the snow.

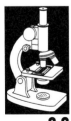

22

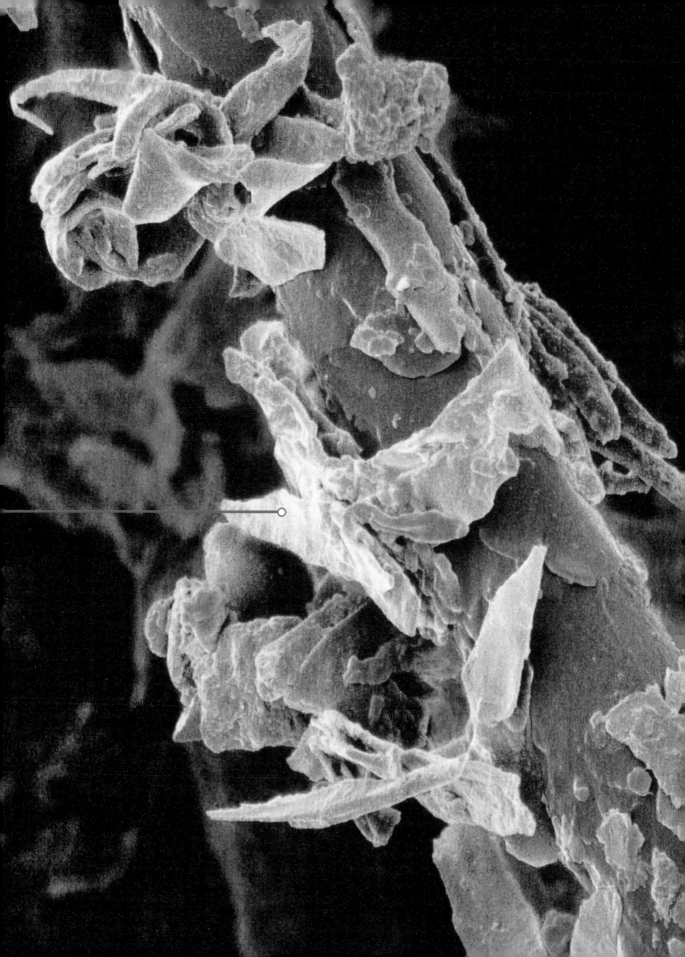

SEEING WITH SOUND

Although some mammals, such as lemurs and flying squirrels, can glide a long way through the air, they are not able to fly like birds. There is only one mammal that can really fly – the bat. Like a bird, the bat has wings and can fly for long distances. But unlike a bird, a bat has skin covered with hair, rather than feathers. These mammals sleep by day and hunt by night. They cannot see very well. They find their way by sending out special sounds. The sounds bounce off objects in their way and send an echo back to the bats, telling them where they are.

Bat hair, like human hair, is made of a material called keratin. It grows from a small pore – called a follicle – located in the upper layer of the skin.

REAL-LIFE VAMPIRES

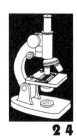

- Most bats eat insects, but a number of them feed only on fruit. Another group of bats feeds on the blood of other animals. They are called vampire bats. After they have pricked the animal's skin, they lap the blood up with their tongue.

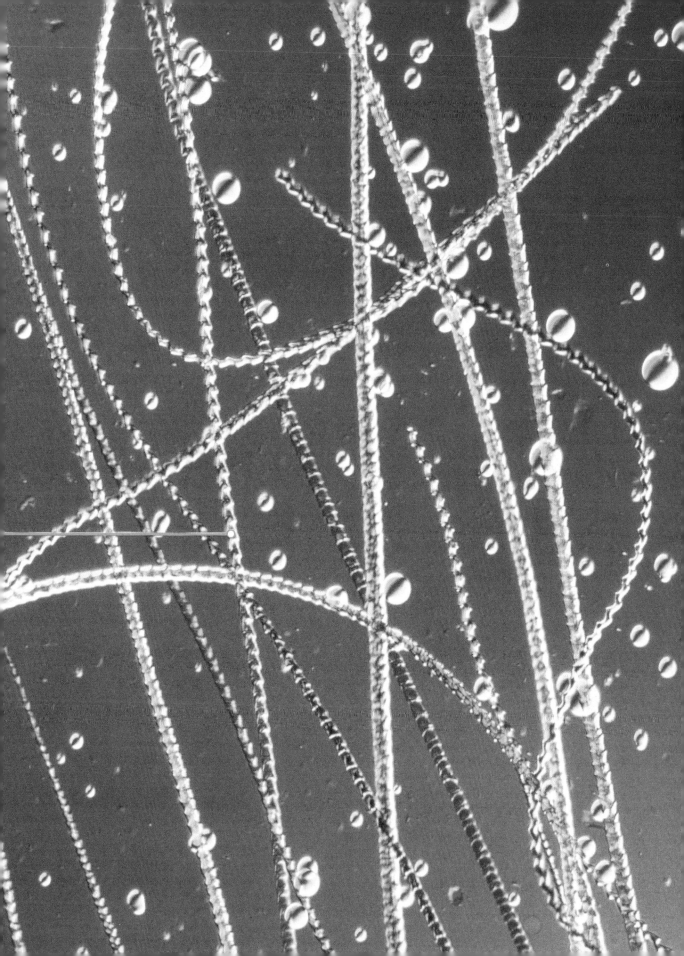

BASIC LIFE FORM

Scientists divide most living things into two main groups: plants and animals. However, there is some living matter that is neither a true plant nor a true animal, but something in between. Protozoa are an example. They are some of the most basic life forms on Earth. Most of them live in water – in the world's oceans, rivers, lakes, streams and ponds. They feed on the waste material from other organisms, on bacteria, algae and other protozoa. The majority of them can move about under their own steam, using whip-like 'limbs' called flagella, or hair-like structures called cilia.

A protozoan (bottom) is about to swallow another protozoan (top). The two rows of fringe-like hairs are the cilia, which help the protozoan to move about.

AMAZING AMOEBAS

• Some protozoa, called amoebas, move in a special way. They can make their bodies into any shape imaginable, and can even make false feet that help them to get from one place to another.

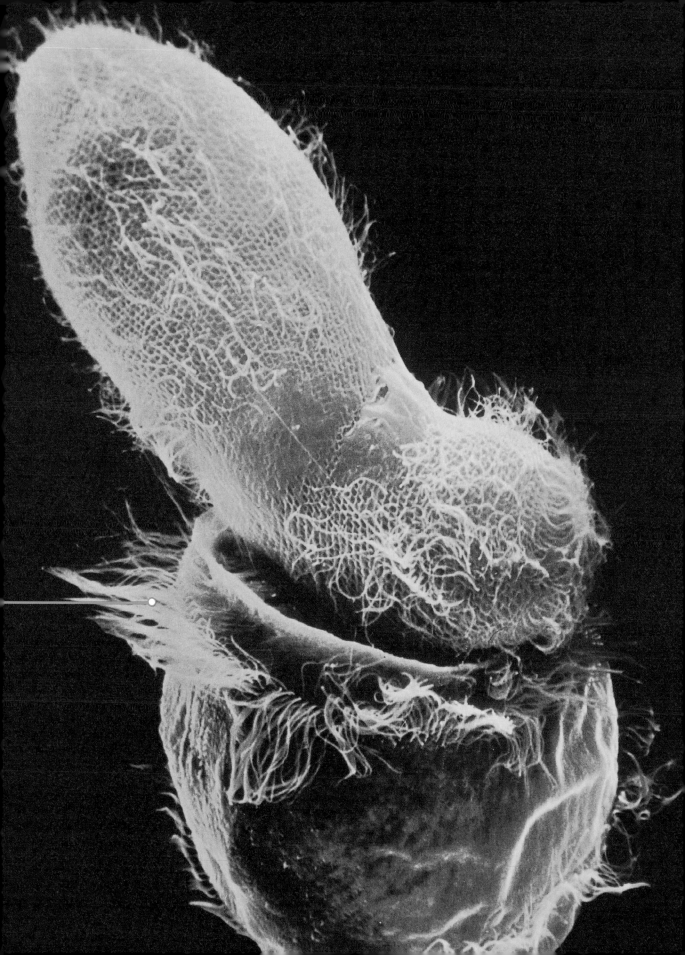

ON THE WING

Most adult insects have wings. These are not modified legs, like the wings of birds, but flat plates of chitin – the tough material that forms the insects' skeleton. These plates are stiffened by rigid veins and hinged to the top of the insect's body. The wings are operated by muscles inside the body, rather like a man sitting in a rowing boat, pulling on the oars. In some insects, including bees and flies, the wings are worked by a vibrating 'lid' on top of the body. Using this system, some small flies can beat their wings at up to 1000 strokes a second.

The wing of a dragonfly is a flat plate of transparent chitin. It has no muscles inside it, as a bird's wing does, but is flicked up and down by muscles inside the insect's body.

TUNING UP

• The drone of a flying insect is made by its vibrating wings. The smaller the insect, the faster its wingbeat, and the higher the note. A small fly beating its wings at 440 strokes per second emits a steady note of A, like a flying tuning fork.

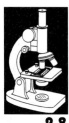

COLOURFUL SCALES

The wings of most types of moths and butterflies are covered with tiny scales arranged like the tiles of a roof. Some of the scales are flat, while others resemble hairs. Beneath the scales the wings are made of chitin – the plastic-like material that forms an insect's skeleton. Some of a moth's wing colour is on the scales themselves, but some of it is produced by light reflecting off the scales. This creates iridescence: the glittering effect also seen on the wings of humming birds. Some moths have no wing scales at all, and their wings are transparent.

The eye-spots on the wings of this Spanish moon moth are usually hidden, but if it is threatened it flashes the 'eyes' to scare its attacker while it makes its escape.

OLD AND BALD

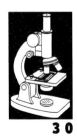

- As a trapped moth beats its wings, it releases clouds of wing scales that look like glittering dust.
- Sometimes a moth or butterfly loses so many wing scales that it goes virtually bald, losing most of its colour in the process.

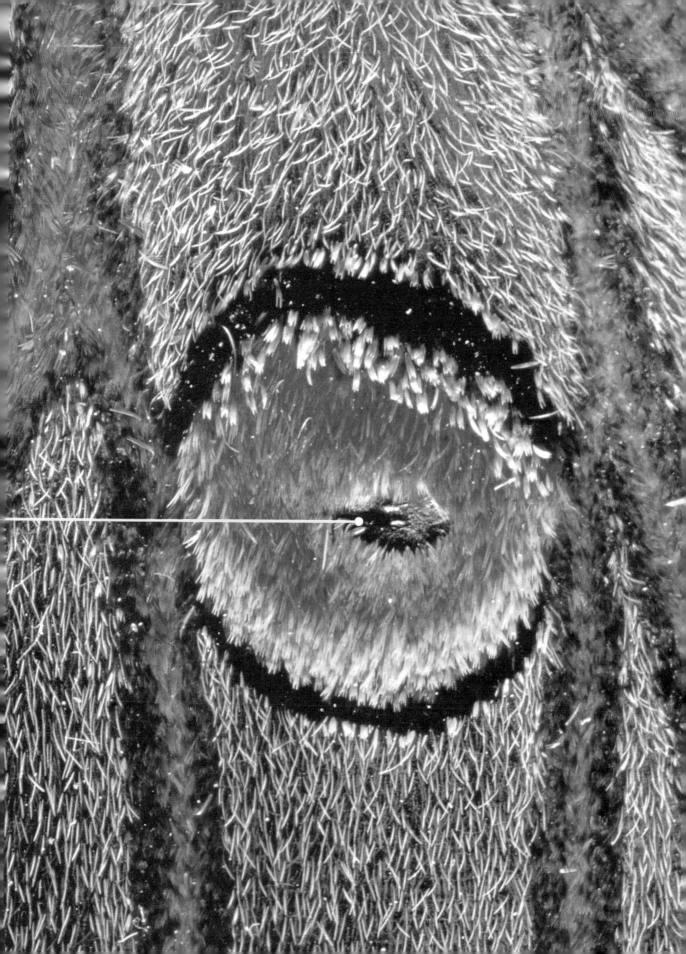

STICKY FEET

How does a fly walk up a window? The answer is, on its feet. As well as two large curved claws for gripping rough surfaces, each of its six feet has two velvety pads. The pads produce a sticky substance that acts rather like low-tack glue. When the fly lands on the window, it presses its footpads onto the glass so they stick. As it walks about, it unpeels the pads of three feet at a time, keeping the other three feet securely glued to the glass. As the fly is very light, this is quite enough to stop it falling off.

The brown pads on the foot of this fly stick to smooth surfaces, while the strong claws grip rough surfaces. The only thing a fly cannot walk over is a spider's web!

SAFETY STRIPES

- Many flies have yellow and black stripes, just like those of stinging bees and wasps. But you can tell the difference, because a fly has only one pair of wings and bees and wasps have two. The flies mimic stinging insects to fool insect-eating birds. The birds see the stripes and leave them alone.

THOUSANDS OF EYES

The eyes of most adult insects are not like ours at all. Instead of having one large lens, each eye is built up from thousands of small lenses. Each lens focuses part of the view on a tiny cluster of sensory cells, which probably detect only brightness and colour. This information is sent to the insect's brain, where all the coloured fragments are built into an image like a picture made of coloured dots. The more lenses there are in the eye, the more dots there are in the picture, which gives more detail. The eyes of a dragonfly may have 30,000 lenses each!

This honeycomb is the eye of a fly, formed from thousands of tiny hexagonal lenses joined together in a curved sheet. Most adult insects have 'compound eyes' like these.

SEE LIKE AN INSECT

- Use a powerful magnifier to look at the picture opposite and you will see that it is made up of many small coloured dots. This is probably the kind of image an insect sees. Each lens in its eye produces a dot, and together all the dots make up a picture.

FEATHERY FEELERS

Many insects have an acute sense of smell. For example, night-flying moths feed on the nectar in flowers. The moths find the flowers by detecting their fragrance, using the scent sensors mounted on the long antennae on their head. Special scents also enable male moths to find females. These scents are called pheromones. The males have feathery antennae which are 'tuned' to the female's pheromones like a radio tuned to a favourite station. This enables some male moths to detect females from over a mile away on a good night.

The antennae of this male night-flying moth bristle with scent detectors. Moths rely on their acute sense of smell to find food and locate other moths in the dark.

DARK FRAGRANCE

- Have you noticed how some flowers, such as honeysuckle, have a stronger scent at night? This is to attract night-flying moths. As the moths feed they carry pollen from one plant to another, fertilizing the flowers and enabling them to produce seeds.

LIQUID LUNCH

Aphids feed by sucking the sap from plants with their needle-like mouthparts, in much the same way as mosquitoes suck blood from humans and animals. The sap is extremely rich in sugar made by the plant leaves, but it contains little protein. The aphids need protein to survive and breed, so to get enough of it they have to drink a lot of sap. This means that they take in much more sugar than they need. They solve the problem by ejecting the surplus sugar as honeydew – the sticky, syrupy substance that often drips onto cars from trees.

A bean aphid plunges its hollow needle into the stem of a plant. Hydraulic pressure inside the plant squirts the sap up the needle and into the aphid's stomach.

HONEYDEW HERDS

- Many types of ants love honeydew, eagerly licking it from the aphids that produce it.
- Some ants keep 'herds' of aphids for their honeydew, gathering them together on selected plants and defending them against enemies.

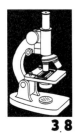

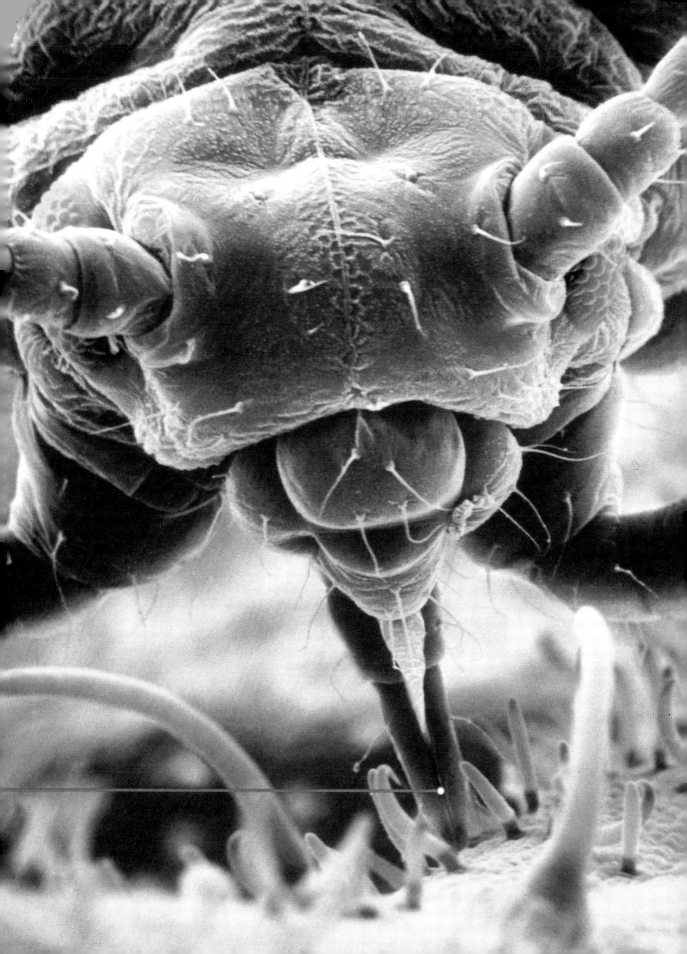

LINKED IN FLIGHT

Some species of flying insects, such as dragonflies, have two pairs of wings that flap independently. In most insects, though, the front and rear wings are linked so they move together as a unit. The linking mechanism varies. The forewings of a butterfly, for example, simply overlap the hindwings so they push them downward on the power stroke. In bees and wasps the wing margins are securely linked together by rows of hooks, so the two pairs of wings act like one pair. The more advanced flies have taken this idea further and abandoned the second pair altogether.

Curved over their linking bar, these hooks lock together the wings of a honeybee while it is in flight, yet slide along the bar so the wings can easily be folded.

AIRBORNE PIONEERS

• The remains of giant dragonflies with 60-cm wingspans have been found fossilized in coal formed over 300 million years ago, long before the first dinosaurs appeared on earth.

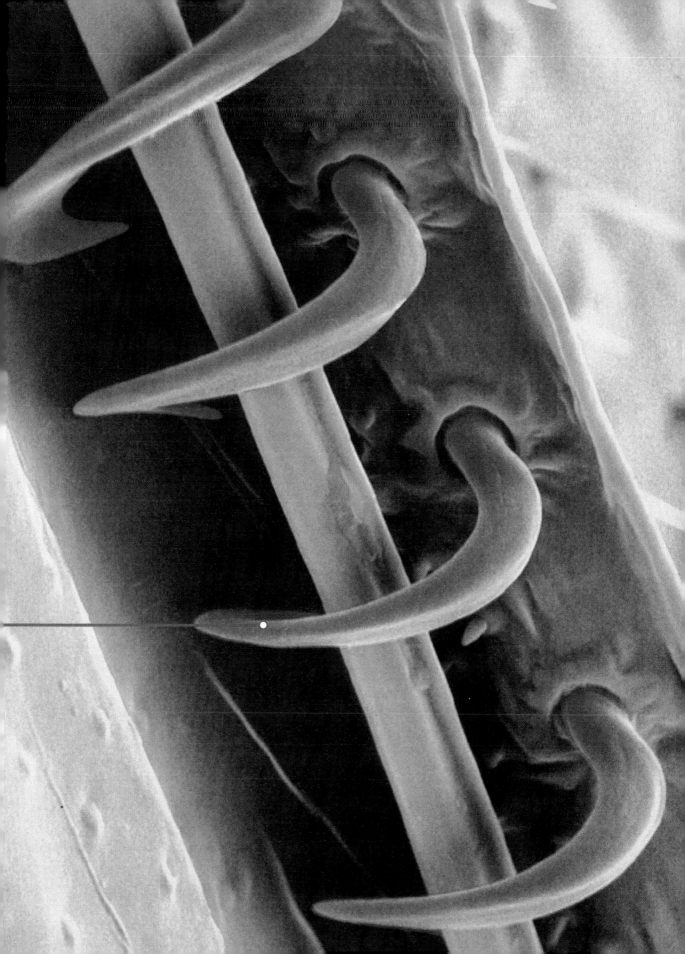

BLOOD-SUCKERS

Not all mosquitoes suck blood. Some types of mosquito hardly ever attack people, and male mosquitoes never do. It is only the female mosquito that bites us, because she needs a meal of blood before she can lay her eggs. She is equipped for bloodsucking with a sharp, hollow 'stylet' like a hypodermic needle. When she plunges this into your skin, the blood surges up it and fills her tiny body. Special substances in her saliva stop the blood from clotting. Just as the bite starts to hurt you, the mosquito pulls out of your skin and makes her getaway – unless you get her first!

The swollen body of this African yellow fever mosquito suggests she has just had a meal. Her needle-like bloodsucking stylet is hidden by a fleshy sheath.

TROPICAL INVADERS

• Some tropical mosquitoes carry dangerous diseases such as malaria and yellow fever. The disease organisms actually live inside the mosquitoes.

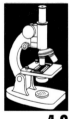

FEEDING ON FRUIT JUICE

Some insects eat plants or other animals, but many cannot manage solid food. They have to find sources of rich, nourishing liquid that they can suck without chewing. Luckily, this is easy for a small animal. The tiny fruit fly, for example, feeds on the juices of rotting fruit, and a small wound on a single fruit can often provide enough food for a whole meal. The fly finds it by sniffing for the sour smell of fermentation, tracks the scent to its source and drinks the fluid through its tube-like mouthparts.

The mouthparts of a fruit fly are adapted into a suction tube so it can pump food-rich fermenting juices into its stomach. It detects the scent of food with its antennae.

INSTRUCTIVE FLIES

- The appearance of every person is determined by a set of instructions which form a pattern on tiny structures called chromosomes. These are normally too small to see, but the chromosomes of the fruit fly are unusually big. This allows scientists to study them and understand how the system works.

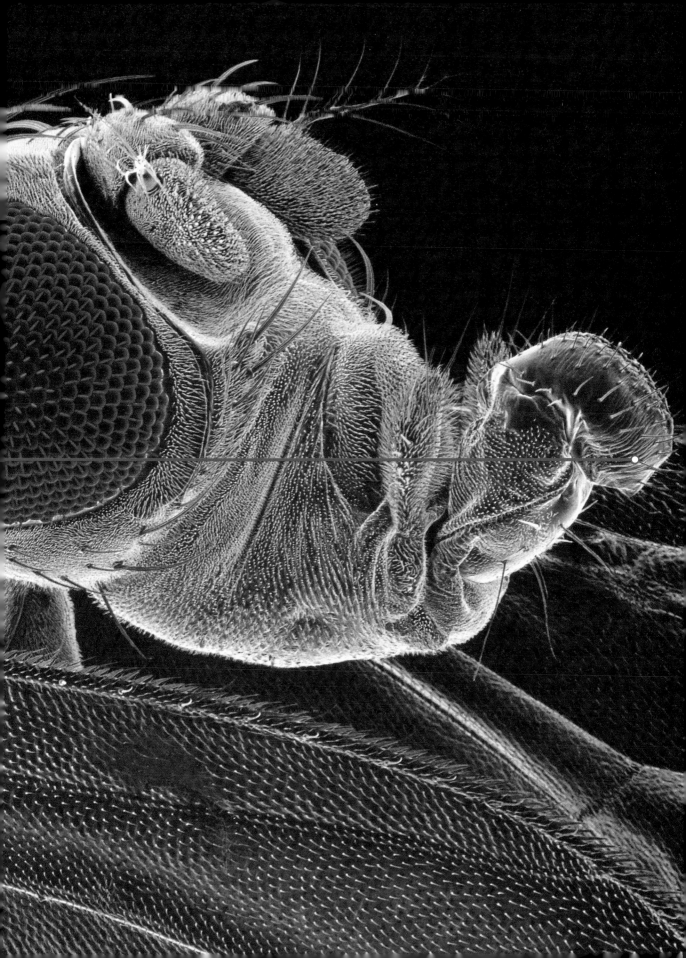

LIVING TO EAT

Many insects go through dramatic changes during their lives. For example, butterflies lay eggs that hatch into caterpillars. A caterpillar is equipped for one thing: eating. It chews its way through enormous quantities of leaves and turns the plant tissue into caterpillar flesh, growing all the time. Eventually it stops eating and develops a protective case called a pupa. Inside the case the caterpillar changes into a butterfly. Eventually the pupa splits and the butterfly crawls out. It flies off, finds a mate and lays some more eggs that will soon hatch into more caterpillars.

This butterfly caterpillar has just chewed its way out of the sculptured egg behind it. It will feed greedily for several weeks and grow to many times its original size.

BRIEF GLORY

• Many adult butterflies cannot eat, and the energy they need for flying is gathered and stored up while they are caterpillars. As butterflies, they live just long enough to produce the next generation, before they run out of fuel and die.

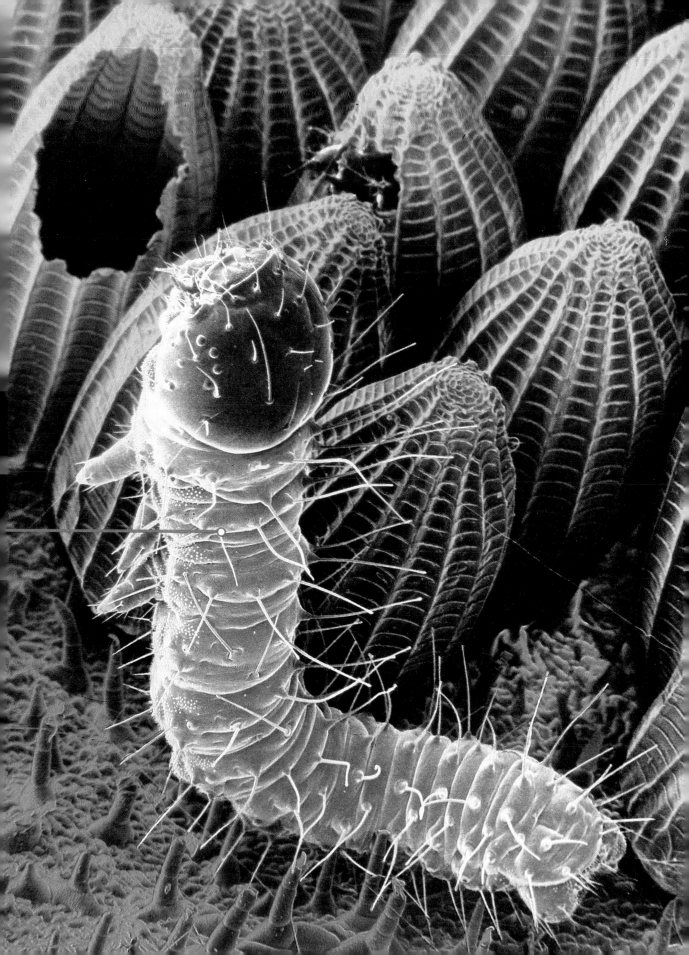

POPULATION EXPLOSION

A newborn aphid emerges from its mother's body – its black eye is just visible. Because it has no father, this aphid will grow into an exact replica of its mother.

Some insects can breed incredibly quickly to make the most of the summer. Aphids such as greenfly and blackfly mate and lay eggs in the autumn. The eggs survive the winter and hatch in spring as females. These 'summer aphids' can produce young without mating. Some may give birth four or five times a day! Within two weeks the young aphids – also females – are producing young at the same rate, until there is a vast aphid population. Finally some males are born in the fall, mate with a special generation of females and produce some more winter eggs.

SAPSUCKERS

• Many aphids lay their winter eggs on woody plants that are often quite unrelated to the lush plants they feed on in summer. The fragrant, white-flowered philadelphus, for example, harbours the eggs of the black bean aphid, or blackfly.

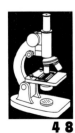

A NASTY BITE

Ants live in enormous colonies like honey bees and yellow-jacket wasps. Each colony has a 'queen' who produces all the eggs, and the other ants in the colony look after her, build the nest and hunt for food. Ants cannot sting, but many have a painful bite. Some also spray a poisonous substance called formic acid at their enemies. This Australian ant, called the bulldog ant, has a particularly nasty bite. It uses its powerful jaws to defend the nest and to hunt for other insects and spiders, which it carries back to the nest as food for the young.

The black bulldog ant of Australia can grow to more than 2 cm long, with jaws to match! Despite its fearsome appearance, the adult ant feeds on sweet plant juices.

SLAVEDRIVERS

- Some ants make 'slaves' of other types of ants by stealing them from their nests when they are young.
- The driver ants of the tropics march in great columns through the forest, killing and eating any animals that can't get out of their way.

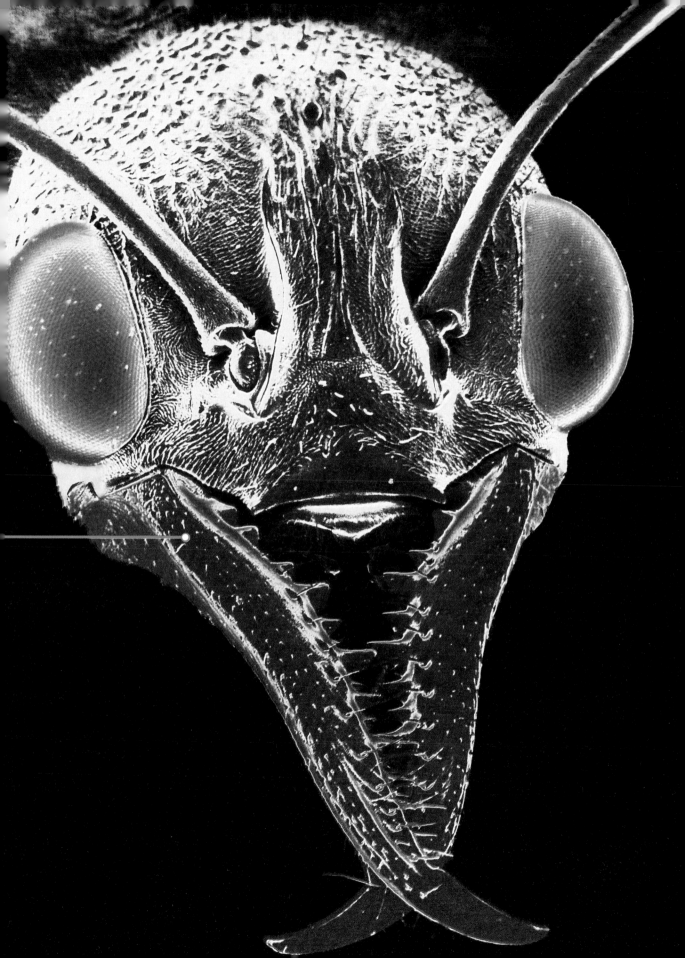

GREEDY GRUBS

Our habit of growing crops in huge fields and storing food in great heaps has turned many insects into pests. The grain weevil, for example, is a type of beetle that feeds on wheat kernels. Using the strong jaws on the end of its slender snout, it bores its way through the tough seed coat and eats the rich flesh within. Females lay their eggs inside the grains, so that when the grubs hatch they have plenty to eat. These activities have little effect on wild wheat, but if the weevils get into a grain store they can multiply very quickly and cause a lot of damage.

The tiny grain weevil grub feeds within a single grain of wheat until it becomes an adult. When the weevil eventually chews its way out it leaves only an empty husk.

SHIP'S BISCUIT

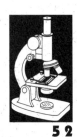

• The stored food eaten by sailors 200 years ago, known as ship's biscuit, was often infested with weevils. The food quality of the biscuit was so bad that the weevils probably improved it by adding to the protein content!

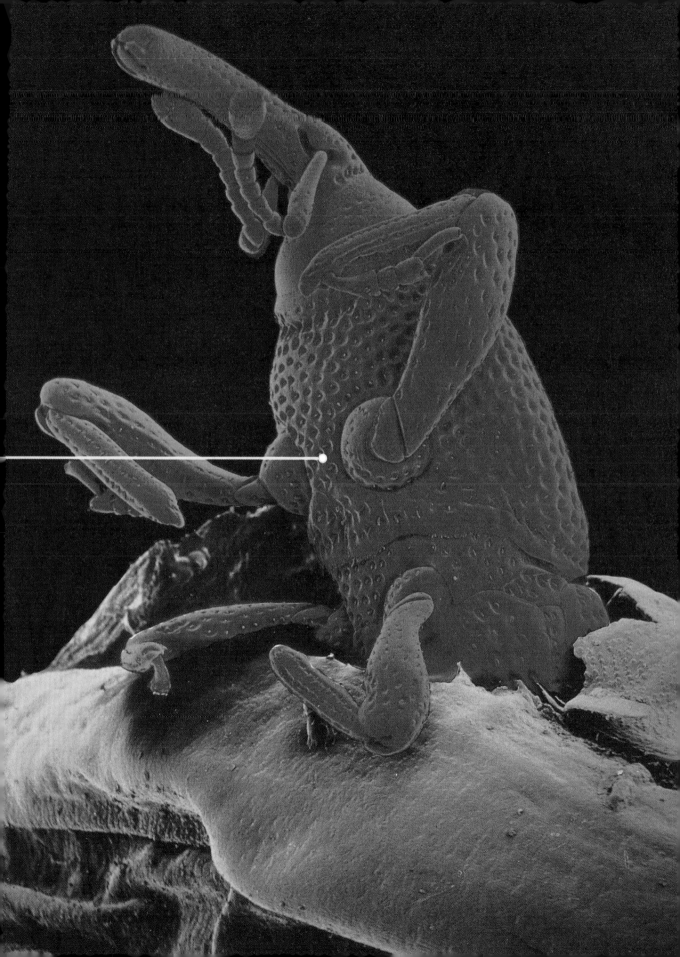

PESTS IN THE GRASS

Most of the tiny, spider-like mites that scurry about in the grass are harmless creatures that feed on debris and other small animals, but in some places there are real pests. Young chigger mites, or red bugs, have a habit of latching onto people and sucking their blood. This causes no trouble in itself, but the saliva of the mite often triggers an allergic reaction, causing an itchy rash that can last for days. In some countries these creatures also carry an organism called Rickettsia, which causes a nasty disease known as scrub-typhus.

Although its young feed on human blood, the adult chigger mite is an active, fierce predator that uses its powerful jaws to kill and eat other microscopic animals.

FINDING A MEAL

- A blood-sucking mite lurking in the backyard senses you are close by detecting the carbon dioxide in the air you breathe out.
- A chigger mite is small enough to slip through the fabric of your clothes, often stopping to feed where a belt or waistband stops it climbing further.

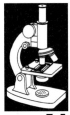

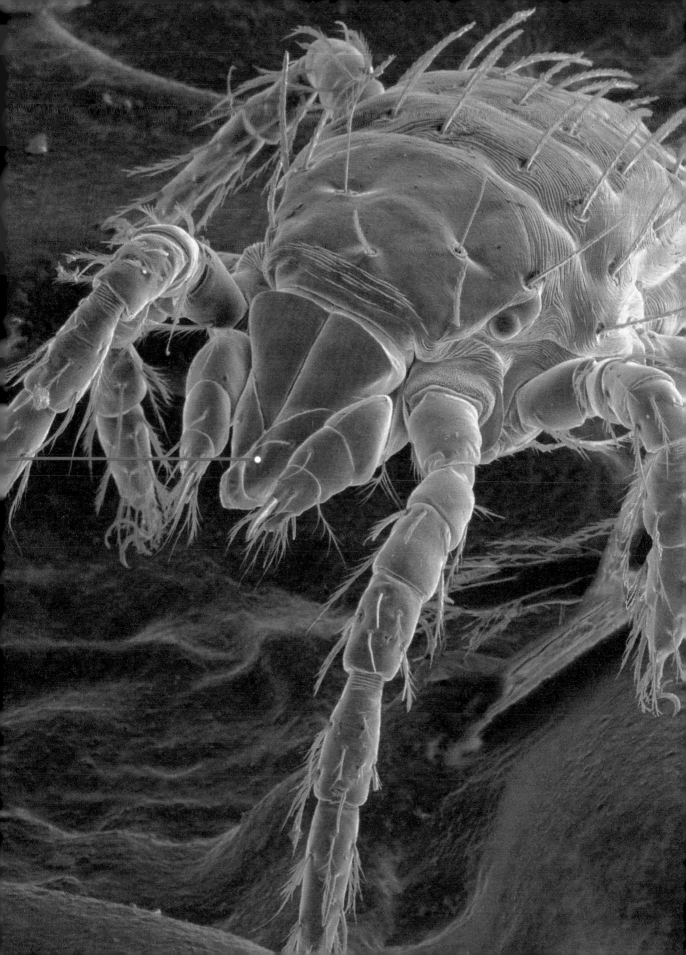

POISONOUS FANGS

There are many kinds of spiders living in our houses and gardens. Some build webs, others live in holes and many just run about – but they all kill and eat other animals. They have big, sharp fangs which they use to inject poison into their victims. The dead animals are often tied up in bundles of silk, and gradually eaten. This is difficult for a spider, because it can swallow only liquid food. It has to pump special substances into its meal that turn it into a kind of soup which the spider can then drink. When it has finished, all that is left of its victim is an empty husk.

Most spiders have eight eyes. The eyes of this web-building spider are very small, so it is almost blind. Its fangs are on the ends of the long jaws under its eyes.

STEEL WEBS

- Spider silk is amazingly strong. A thread of spider silk is stronger than steel wire of the same thickness.
- A spider always build its web in the same way, following a sequence like a computer programme that is loaded into its brain at birth.

LIFE IN THE SOIL

Fertile soil teems with millions of tiny animals. These feed on dead plant and animal matter, and help the processes of decay that turn dead things into food for living plants. Two of these soil animals are shown here: a mite and a nematode worm. Mites are like microscopic spiders. They have eight legs and very strong jaws for chewing their food. There are at least 30,000 different types found almost everywhere. Nematodes are tiny worms that have smooth, cylindrical bodies. There are at least 80,000 types of nematode, but they only live in damp places.

A nematode worm investigates a meal mite – a close encounter between two of the millions of microscopic animals living in every square metre of the soil.

TINY KILLERS

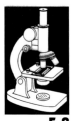

- Although the microscopic animals living in the soil do a lot of good, some mites and nematodes are harmful. Nematodes found in tropical countries may live inside the bodies of animals – including humans – feeding on body tissues and causing diseases.

BLIND BURROWER

The soil in your backyard is largely formed by the action of earthworms. These useful animals spend their lives tunnelling through the earth and swallowing it to absorb any food particles. The tunnels allow air into the ground and help prevent it getting waterlogged. The earthworms eject the waste soil near the surface, so they are constantly bringing up soil from below. This soil is rich in plant foods that have been washed down by rain water, so it is vital for the health of many plants. Where there are no earthworms the soil is infertile, and many plants cannot survive.

An earthworm has a strong snout for forcing its way through the soil, but it has no eyes. Despite this it can sense the light, and always burrows away from it.

SINKING STONES

• Earthworms burrow beneath stones, so the stones gradually sink into the ground. They cannot swallow stones so the soil they eject on the surface is stone-free. If you dig out a piece of grassland, you will see the stone-free layer made by earthworms.

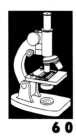

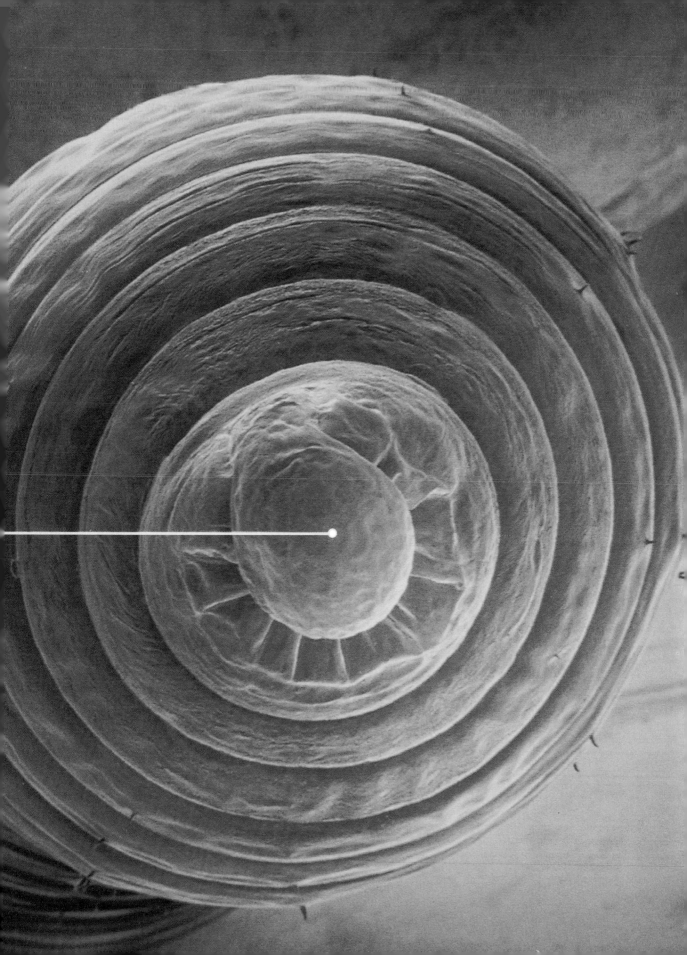

LYING IN WAIT

Many forest animals are attacked by tiny blood-sucking parasites called ticks. A tick must have a meal of blood before it can breed. Looking rather like miniature spiders, ticks lurk in the undergrowth waiting for warm-blooded animals like deer to brush past. A female tick may survive for anything up to seven years before she gets her chance to climb onto a victim, bite through its skin and push her barbed snout into the wound. As the tick steadily pumps the blood into her body, it inflates until it looks like a shiny blue pea. When she can take no more she drops off and begins to lay her eggs.

The barbed snout of this deer tick allows it to cling to the skin of its host and suck its blood for several days without any danger of being brushed off.

DISEASE CARRIERS

- Ticks can feed off people, and are extremely difficult to remove once they are attached.
- Ticks in some countries carry dangerous diseases such as Rocky Mountain spotted fever, which may be fatal.

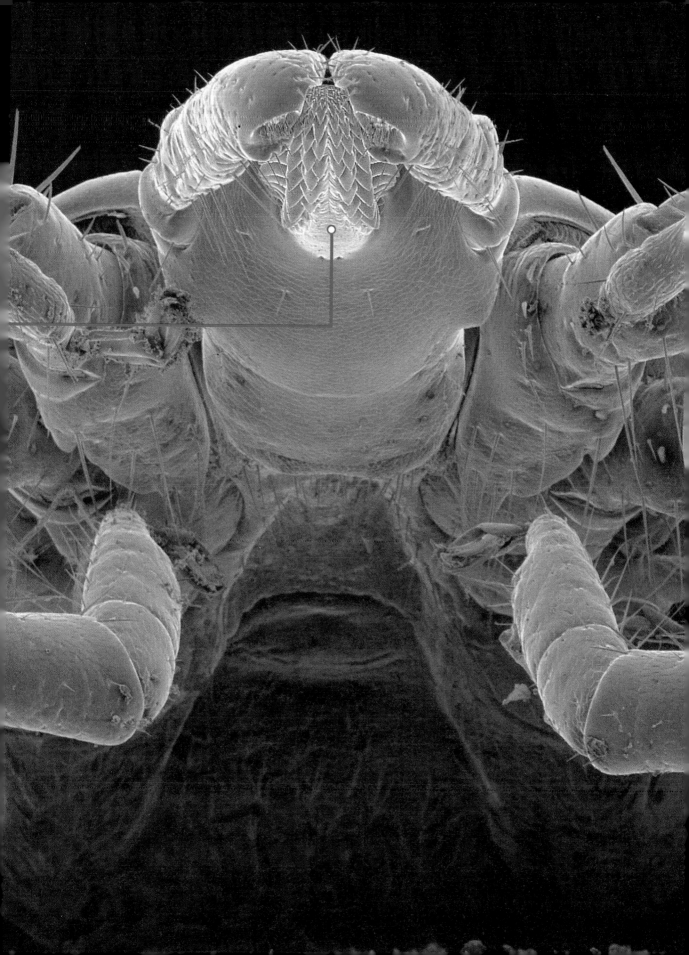

INDEX

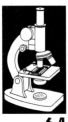

64